The Wild West!
A Kid's Guide To California's Calico Ghost Town

Photography by John D. Weigand
Poetry by Penelope Dyan

Bellissima Publishing, LLC
Jamul, California
www.bellissimapublishing.com

Copyright © 2014 by Penny D. Weigand and John D. Weigand

All rights reserved. No part of this book may be reproduced or transmitted in any form or by any means, electronic or mechanical, including photocopying, recording, or by any other means, or by any information or storage retrieval system, without permission from the publisher.

ISBN 978-1-61477-168-5
First Edition

"Are ghosts real? And if they are real,
do they just happen to live in ghost towns?"

Penelope Dyan

The Wild West!
Bellissima Publishing, LLC

Introduction

There is a very fun stop on the way back to Los Angeles, California from Las Vegas, Nevada, right off the I-15; and that stop is none other than Calico Ghost Town! Whether you are a kid or a grown-up, it's a great place to stretch your legs, pick up a souvenir or two and get something to eat!

The town of Calico was built during an 1881 silver strike. It was the largest silver find ever found in California. Calico boomed until the mines began to go dry in 1896. By 1904 it was a ghost town. Walter Knott purchased Calico in the 1950s, and architecturally restored all but five remaining original buildings to look exactly as they did in the 1880s. Today it is a County Park.

Written by Penelope Dyan, award winning author, attorney and former teacher, with photographs by John D. Weigand, this learn to read book is perfect to carry along on your road trip, or it can be used simply to practice reading skills. Then look for the free music video that goes along with this book, on the Bellissimavideo YouTube channel for even more learning fun!

The Wild West!
Bellissima Publishing, LLC

The Wild West!
A Kid's Guide To Californa's Calico Ghost Town

Photography by John D. Weigand
Poetry by Penelope Dyan

You approach Calico, turning off I-15, and you spot a hole in the ground. Your dad says, "That might be a place where silver was once found! Or maybe it was a hideout for a guy named Ace, who cheated at cards, and tried to shoot out this place!"

You get closer as you drive up
the wind of the road.
Calico was built in 1881, you are told.
You see a parking sign as you get near.
Your mom says,
"You're in for some fun today,
My dear!"

Inside Calico you find a place
with a post office,
that has groceries and meats.
You buy some candy and soda here
and some other fun treats.

Mom goes inside the Candle company and she buys a candle or two, but that isn't the sort of thing that has ANY interest for you!

THEN you see a restaurant!
there is a Fire Station next door.
You are ALL still hungry and thirsty,
so you DECIDE to eat MORE!
It's very hot out here.
It's the desert, you see.
And a nice cool restaurant
is a GREAT place to be!
As your mother rests her weary feet,
you all go inside
and have something to eat!

On a high hill you see a shack.
Your dad says,
"Now that was really built way back!"
You wonder about the days of old,
and you think about all of the stories
that you have been told.
You think about
that hole in the ground!
And you wonder how the miners spent
all the silver that was found!
A sign on the shack says "hideout,"
and you decide this must be the place
where that guy hid out
whose name was Ace!

You see a hotel,
as you look all around.
You wonder if there really ARE ghosts
in THIS old ghost town.
Maybe Ace is playing cards inside;
because now that he's a ghost,
he doesn't NEED to hide!

You see a sign that points the way,
you decide that THIS
is a most glorious, and FUN day!
And so you leave that guy named Ace
far, far behind,
wondering what else you might find.

There it is!
You dad says you can explore
inside the Maggie Mine,
and you think THAT idea
is mighty, mighty fine!
So up the dusty steps
to the Maggie Mining Company
you all walk.
and about the history of Calico,
you talk and talk!

There is a mining tunnel to explore.
There is a re-created mining office
And there is even more!.

There is an old time train
right outside,
and the conductor will tell
you some more history of this place
as you ride!
And as you go chug, chug, chugging
down that track,
you are having so much FUN,
that you NEVER want to go back!
But as around the bend you wend,
you know that ALL things
(both good AND bad)
MUST come to an end!

And then, as you disembark the train,
you spot an old time Chinese bath.
You read the words on the tub,
and you laugh and you laugh!
You wonder what it would be like
to take off your clothes,
(to have nothing on beneath your nose)
and to hop right into that old tub,
and then to pay ten cents
to get a full Chinese scrub!

Before you leave Calico,
you can also take a picture or two.
(It's free!)
And I would most definitely do it
if I were YOU!
Or you COULD go back
and you COULD buy a scrub,
and you COULD sit right down
in that old Chinese tub!

"Our history, although short in comparison to others, is certainly well worth preserving."

Penelope Dyan

www.ingramcontent.com/pod-product-compliance
Ingram Content Group UK Ltd.
Pitfield, Milton Keynes, MK11 3LW, UK
UKHW060136240426
12048UKWH00002B/64